Kooking with the Kardashians

40 Reality Star Recipes

By

Angel Burns

License Notices

This book or parts thereof might not be reproduced in any format for personal or commercial use without the written permission of the author. Possession and distribution of this book by any means without said permission is prohibited by law.

All content is for entertainment purposes and the author accepts no responsibility for any damages, commercially or personally, caused by following the content.

Get Your Daily Deals Here!

Free books on me! Subscribe now to receive free and discounted books directly to your email. This means you will always have choices of your next book from the comfort of your own home and a reminder email will pop up a few days beforehand, so you never miss out! Every day, free books will make their way into your inbox and all you need to do is choose what you want.

What could be better than that?

Fill out the box below to get started on this amazing offer and start receiving your daily deals right away!

https://angel-burns.gr8.com

Table of Contents

Homemade Kardashian Recipes

HHHHHHHHHHHHHHHHHHHHHHHHHHHHHHHHHHHHHHHHHHH

Chapter I – Kendall and Kylie

HHHHHHHHHHHHHHHHHHHHHHHHHHHHHHHHHHHHHHHH

Recipe 1: Kylie Grilled Cheese

Kylie spices-up a regular grilled cheese sandwich with lashings of hot sauce. It might not be a gourmet meal but never the less if Kylie says it's good, then it's good.

Yield: 1

Preparation Time: 10mins

Ingredient List:

- Butter
- 2 slices sourdough bread
- 2 slices of American cheese
- Salt and black pepper
- Hot sauce (to serve)

HHHHHHHHHHHHHHHHHHHHHHHHHHHHHHHHHHHHHHHH

Instructions:

1. Add a generous knob of butter to a pan over moderate heat.

2. Once melted, add the bread to the pan.

3. Add a cheese slice to each piece of bread and season with salt and black pepper.

4. Combine the 2 slices of bread and flip over. The sandwich is ready when the cheese is gooey.

5. Serve with hot sauce.

Recipe 2: Grilled Chicken and Rice

Although Kendall does occasionally spoil herself, she also likes to eat healthily, and grilled chicken with rice is the perfect option for anyone watching their weight. What's more, instant rice and ready-to-use chicken, means that it's also super quick to prepare.

Yield: 4

Preparation Time: 12mins

Ingredient List:

- 1 cup instant-cook rice
- 1 cup chicken stock
- ½ cup frozen green pepper (thawed, chopped)
- ¼ cup onion (peeled, chopped)
- 2 teaspoons olive oil
- 1 (9 ounce) package ready-to-use grilled chicken breast strips
- ½ cup frozen peas (thawed)
- ½ cup frozen corn (thawed)
- 1 teaspoon rubbed sage
- 1 teaspoon basil
- ⅛ teaspoons salt
- ⅛ teaspoons pepper

HHHHHHHHHHHHHHHHHHHHHHHHHHHHHHHHHHHHHHH

Instructions:

1. Cook the instant rice in the chicken stock according to the package instructions.

2. In the meantime, in a large frying pan, fry the green pepper and onion in olive oil, until crisp-tender, for 2-3 minutes.

3. Add the chicken followed by the peas, corn, sage, and basil stirring to combine.

4. Cook, while uncovered for 4-5 minutes over moderate heat, until heated through.

5. Stir in the rice and season with $1\frac{1}{8}$ teaspoon each of salt and pepper.

Recipe 3: Baked Avocado Eggs

Forget the pancakes! Kendall enjoys a model breakfast of avocado and eggs. Not only is it extremely healthy but also very satisfying.

Yield: 2

Preparation Time: 25mins

Ingredient List:

- 2 small eggs
- 1 ripe avocado (peeled, pitted, halved)
- 2 teaspoons fresh chives (chopped)
- 1 teaspoon fresh parsley (chopped)
- Pinch of sea salt
- Dash of black pepper
- 2 slices lean bacon (cooked, crumbled)

HHHHHHHHHHHHHHHHHHHHHHHHHHHHHHHHHHHHHHHH

Instructions:

1. Preheat the main oven to 425 degrees F.

2. Carefully, keeping the yolks intact, crack the eggs into a bowl.

3. Place the halves of avocado in a casserole dish. Arrange them around the edge of the dish to ensure that the slices don't fall over.

4. Gently spoon one egg yolk into the hole left by the avocado pit.

5. Continue spooning the egg white into the hole until it is filled. Repeat the process with the remaining yolk, and white.

6. Season each of the filled avocadoes with chive, parsley, salt, and black pepper.

7. Place the casserole dish in the oven and bake for 15 minutes, until the eggs are cooked through.

8. Scatter the crumbled bacon over the top and serve.

Recipe 4: The Model American Bacon Cheeseburger

Surprisingly, Kendall cites the classic burger as one of her top three favorite foods. This girl has taste!

Yield: 4

Preparation Time: 30mins

Ingredient List:

- 2 tablespoons onion (peeled, finely chopped)
- 2 tablespoons ketchup
- 1 garlic clove (peeled, minced)
- 1 teaspoon sugar
- 1 teaspoon Worcestershire sauce
- 1 teaspoon steak sauce
- ¼ teaspoons cider vinegar
- 1 pound ground beef
- 4 slices sharp Cheddar cheese
- 4 hamburger buns (split, toasted)
- 8 cooked bacon strips

Toppings:

- Lettuce leaves
- Tomato (sliced)
- Onion (sliced)

HHHHHHHHHHHHHHHHHHHHHHHHHHHHHHHHHHHHHH

Instructions:

1. In a bowl combine the onion, ketchup, garlic, sugar, Worcestershire sauce, steak sauce, cider vinegar, and ground beef, mixing well to fully incorporate.

2. Shape the mixture into 4 patties.

3. Covered, grill the burgers over moderate heat for between 47 minutes on each side, depending on your preference.

4. Top each burger with a slice of cheese and grill for 60 seconds, or until entirely melted.

5. Serve the cheeseburgers on the toasted buns, loading each one with 2 slices of bacon and your choice of toppings.

Recipe 5: Candied Yams

Kylie is a real soul sister when it comes to cooking yams. She says that this recipe featuring lots of spices and sugar is one of her all-time favorites.

Yield: 4-6

Preparation Time: 1hour 5mins

Ingredient List:

- 8 tablespoons salted butter
- 1 cup granulated sugar
- ¼ cup brown sugar
- 1 teaspoon ground cinnamon
- ½ teaspoons ground nutmeg
- ¼ teaspoons ground ginger
- ¼ teaspoons ground cloves
- 1 tablespoon pure vanilla essence
- 5 medium yams (washed, peeled, chopped to ½" thick pieces)

HHHHHHHHHHHHHHHHHHHHHHHHHHHHHHHHHHHHHH

Instructions:

1. Place the yams in a 9x13" casserole dish.

2. Over moderate heat, melt the butter in a pan.

3. Once melted, add the white and brown sugars followed by the cinnamon, nutmeg, ginger, and cloves.

4. Turn the heat off and stir in the vanilla essence.

5. Pour the candied mixture over the yams, making sure they are evenly coated.

6. Cover the casserole dish with aluminum foil and bake in the oven for half an hour.

7. Remove the dish from the oven and baste the yams with the candied mixture.

8. Replace the foil and bake for an additional 15-20 minutes.

9. Remove from the oven and allow to rest for several minutes before serving.

Recipe 6: Sushi Rolls

Kylie is a huge fan of sushi, and these California sushi rolls are as good as any high-end restaurant.

Yield: 64 pieces

Preparation Time: 1hour

Ingredient List:

- 2 cups sushi rice (rinsed, drained)
- Water
- ¼ cup rice vinegar
- 2 tablespoons sugar
- ½ teaspoons salt
- 2 tablespoons sesame seeds (toasted)
- 2 tablespoons black sesame seeds
- 3 ounces imitation crabmeat (julienned)
- 1 medium-ripe avocado (peeled, pitted, julienned)
- Reduced-sodium soy sauce
- Store-bought wasabi
- Pickled ginger slices
- Special equipment:
- Bamboo sushi mat
- 8 nori sheets

HHHHHHHHHHHHHHHHHHHHHHHHHHHHHHHHHHHHHHHH

Instructions:

1. In a large pan, combine the rice with water and allow to stand for half an hour. Bring to boil. Turn the heat down to low, cover with a lid and simmer for between 15-20 minutes, until the rice is fork tender and the water is absorbed.

2. Remove the pan from the heat and allow to stand, while covered for 10 minutes.

3. In the meantime, in a bowl, combine the vinegar with the sugar and salt, constantly stirring until the sugar is entirely dissolved.

4. Transfer the rice to a shallow bowl, and drizzle with the vinegar mixture.

5. Using a wooden spoon, in a slicing movement, stir the rice to enable it to slightly cool.

6. Cover with a clean damp cloth; this will help it to remain moist. The rice can be prepared up to 2 hours in advance and stored at room temperature if covered with a damp cloth. Do not refrigerate.

7. Scatter the toasted and black sesame seeds onto a serving plate and set to one side.

8. Arrange the sushi mat on a clean work surface, so that the mat rolls facing away from you, line with kitchen wrap.

9. Place ¾ cup of rice on the kitchen wrap and with damp fingers, gently form the rice into an 8" square.

10. Top the rice with 1 nori sheet. Place a little bit of crab and avocado approximately 1½" from the bottom edge of the nori sheet.

11. Roll the rice mixture up over the filling, using the bamboo mat to lift and compress the mixture while you roll. Remove the kitchen wrap as you roll.

12. Remove the mat and roll the sushi rolls in the sesame seeds.

13. Cover with kitchen wrap.

14. Repeat the process with the remaining ingredients to create 8 rolls. Slice each one into 8 portions.

15. Serve the rolls with soy sauce, wasabi and slices of ginger.

Recipe 7: Fettucine with Peas

Kendall reveals that in her opinion she cooks this dish of pasta and peas better than anyone else in her family!

Yield: 4

Preparation Time: 17mins

Ingredient List:

- 16 ounces fettuccine
- ½ onion (peeled, chopped)
- 4 ounces frozen peas
- 1 clove garlic (peeled, minced)
- ¼ cup Parmesan (freshly grated)
- Salt and ground pepper
- ½ fresh lemon

HHHHHHHHHHHHHHHHHHHHHHHHHHHHHHHHHHHHHHHH

Instructions:

1. Over moderate heat, cook the fettuccine until al dente. Reserve 1 cup of pasta cooking water.

2. In a pan, fry the onions until softened. Add the peas and garlic and fry for an additional 3 minutes.

3. Stir in the cheese along with the drained pasta, moistening with a tablespoon or two, as needed, with the reserved pasta cooking water.

4. Toss to combine and season with salt, pepper, and a squeeze of fresh lemon juice.

Recipe 8: Mexican Tacos

Mexican food is another of Kylie's go-to meals. She loves guacamole, and when she spends time in LA, she is a regular visitor to its many Mexican restaurants. Nothing, however, can beat homemade tacos.

Yield: 4

Preparation Time: 30mins

Ingredient List:

- 1 pound lean ground beef
- 1 medium onion (peeled, finely chopped)
- 1 garlic clove (peeled, minced)
- ½ cup water
- 1 tablespoon chili powder
- 1½ teaspoons ground cumin
- ½ teaspoons salt
- ½ teaspoons paprika
- ½ teaspoons pepper
- ¼ teaspoons dried oregano
- ¼ teaspoons crushed red pepper flakes
- 8 taco shells (warm)

Toppings:

- Lettuce (shredded)
- Tomatoes (chopped)
- Green onions (sliced)
- Cheddar cheese (shredded)

HHHHHHHHHHHHHHHHHHHHHHHHHHHHHHHHHHHHHHHH

Instructions:

1. In a large frying pan or skillet, cook the beef together with the onion and garlic over moderate heat until the meat is no longer pink; drain well

2. Stir in the water along with the chili powder, ground cumin, salt, paprika, pepper, dried oregano, and red pepper flakes. Bring to a boil.

3. Turn the heat down; simmer, while uncovered, for between 5-10 minutes until thickened.

4. Spoon the beef mixture into the warm taco shells.

5. Top with toppings of your choice and enjoy.

Recipe 9: Kendall's Chunky Guacamole

Kendall loves guacamole and tortilla chips. In fact, it's one of the foods the model keeps in her dressing room.

Yield: 2-4

Preparation Time: 8mins

Ingredient List:

- 2 ripe avocados (peeled, pitted)
- ½ teaspoons kosher salt
- 1 tablespoon freshly squeezed lime juice
- ¼ cup red onion (peeled, minced)
- 1-2 Serrano chilies (seeded, minced)
- 2 tablespoons cilantro leaves and stems (finely chopped)
- Black pepper
- ½ ripe tomato (seeds, pulp removed, chopped)
- Tortilla chips (to serve)

HHHHHHHHHHHHHHHHHHHHHHHHHHHHHHHHHHHHHHHH

Instructions:

1. Using a fork, mash the avocado to a chunky consistency.

2. Add the salt along with the fresh lime juice; this will prevent the avocado from discoloring.

3. Add the red onion, chilies, cilantro, black pepper, and tomato. The number of peppers will depend on your preferred level of heat.

4. Cover with kitchen wrap and place in the fridge, to chill.

5. Serve with tortilla chips and enjoy.

Recipe 10: Lemon Fro-Yo

This tangy citrus FroYo is the perfect dessert or treat, and according to Kendall, she could eat it every single day. She does, however, like to go Greek!

Yield: 5 cups

Preparation Time: 4hours 30mins

Ingredient List:

- 4 cups plain Greek yogurt
- 1⅔ cups sugar
- ⅓ cup freshly squeezed lemon juice
- 1 tablespoon lemon peel (grated)
- 4 drops of yellow food coloring

HHHHHHHHHHHHHHHHHHHHHHHHHHHHHHHHHHHHHHHH

Instructions:

1. In a mixing bowl, combine the yogurt with the sugar, fresh lemon juice, and grated peel, mixing to combine.

2. Stir in the yellow food coloring.

3. Pour the mixture into an ice cream churner and process according to the manufacturer's directions.

4. Transfer the fro-yo to freezer containers, leaving a little headspace to allow for expansion.

5. Freeze until firm, 2-4 hours.

Recipe 11: Kylie's Special Fried Chicken

This recipe is, according to Kylie's friend the bomb! And who doesn't like fried chicken for girl's night in watching reality TV shows?

Yield: 4

Preparation Time: 35mins

Ingredient List:

- 1¾ cups all-purpose flour
- 1 tablespoon dried thyme
- 1 tablespoon paprika
- 2 teaspoons salt
- 2 teaspoons garlic powder
- 1 teaspoon pepper
- 1 large egg
- ⅓ cup whole milk
- 2 tablespoons freshly squeezed lemon juice
- 1 (4 pound) fryer/broiler chicken (separate into pieces)
- Oil (for frying)

HHHHHHHHHHHHHHHHHHHHHHHHHHHHHHHHHHHHH

Instructions:

1. In a shallow dish, combine the flour, thyme, paprika, salt, garlic, and pepper.

2. In a second shallow dish, whisk the egg, milk and fresh lemon juice until combined.

3. Dip the chicken first in the flour mixture, coating all sides and shaking off any excess.

4. Second, dip the chicken in the egg, then once again in the flour.

5. In a deep fryer, heat the oil to a temperature of 375 degrees F.

6. In batches, fry the chicken for between 6-10 minutes on each side until the chicken's juices run clear and they are golden brown.

7. Drain the fried chicken on kitchen paper towels.

Chapter II – Khloe and Kourtney

HHHHHHHHHHHHHHHHHHHHHHHHHHHHHHHHHHHHHHH

Recipe 12: Wild Salmon with a Balsamic Glaze

Khole's nutritionist recommends that in order to promote sleep and reduce inflammation it is advisable to increase your intake of Omega fatty acids. You can do this by eating more fish for your evening meal. Recommended fish include Arctic char, sea bass, and salmon.

Yield: 1

Preparation Time: 40mins

Ingredient List:

- Extra virgin olive oil
- 4 ounces filet wild-caught salmon
- Sea salt
- ½ cup Brussels sprouts (sliced into quarters)
- 2 cups organic spinach

Glaze:

- ⅓ cup balsamic vinegar
- 1 teaspoon raw honey

HHHHHHHHHHHHHHHHHHHHHHHHHHHHHHHHHHHHHHHH

Instructions:

1. Preheat the grill to moderate heat.

2. Brush a small amount of oil onto the salmon fillet and season with a pinch of salt.

3. Skin side, facing upwards, grill the salmon for approximately 5 minutes.

4. Gently flip the salmon over and allow to cook for an additional 3-5 minutes.

5. Remove the salmon from the grill and very gently remove the skin.

6. Cover the salmon, keep warm and set to one side.

7. Add the Brussels sprouts to a pan, lightly drizzle with oil and add a pinch of salt. Sauté for 7-10 minutes, until golden.

8. Add the balsamic vinegar to the pan and bring to boil, before reducing to a simmer.

9. Cook for approximately 12-15 minutes, until the mixture, has a syrup-like consistency.

10. Remove the pan from the heat and stir in the honey along with a pinch of salt.

11. Arrange the salmon on top of a bed of spinach.

12. Top with the Brussels sprouts and drizzle with the glaze.

Recipe 13: Kourtney Kardashian's Go-To Detox Salmon Salad

When Kourtney is on a health kick, she looks to this light, protein-packed de-tox salad with omega-3 rich salmon.

Yield: 2-4

Preparation Time: 35mins

Ingredient List:

Salad:

- Freshly squeezed juice from 1 lemon
- 1 pound skinless, center-cut salmon
- Himalayan sea salt and fresh ground black pepper
- 2 tablespoons olive oil
- 3 hearts of romaine lettuce (coarsely chopped)
- 1 cucumber (peeled, diced)
- 2 carrots (peeled, diced)
- 1 large avocado (peeled, pitted, diced)

Dressing:

- ⅛ cup rice wine vinegar
- 1 shallot clove (diced)
- 1 teaspoon Himalayan salt
- ⅛ teaspoons freshly ground black pepper
- 2 teaspoons tahini
- 1 tablespoon sesame seeds
- ½ cup sesame oil

HHHHHHHHHHHHHHHHHHHHHHHHHHHHHHHHHHHHHHHH

Instructions:

1. To prepare the salad. Drizzle the fresh juice from the lemon over the salmon before seasoning with salt and pepper. Set aside for 10 minutes.

2. Over moderate heat, heat 2 tablespoons of olive oil.

3. Add the salmon to the pan and cook for 4 minutes, until the fish is opaque. Flip over once, and cook for an additional 4 minutes.

4. Transfer the salmon to a plate and allow to rest for 5 minutes.

5. Add the romaine lettuce to a glass salad bowl.

6. Add the cucumber and carrots to the salad followed by the salmon.

7. Drizzle the dressing over the salad and garnish with diced avocado.

8. To prepare the dressing, combine the wine vinegar with the shallot clove, salt, black pepper, tahini, sesame seeds, and sesame oil, whisking until incorporated.

9. Use as directed.

Recipe 14: Chicken and Dumplings

Mum Kris says that Khloe is the best cook in the family and she likes nothing more than making a family dinner of chicken and dumplings, even if it does take six hours to prepare.

Yield: 8

Preparation Time: 6hours 25mins

Ingredient List:

- 6 boneless skinless chicken thighs (chopped)
- ½ teaspoons salt (divided)
- ½ teaspoons pepper (divided)
- 1 tablespoon canola oil
- 3 celery ribs (chopped)
- 2 medium carrots (peeled, chopped)
- 1 large onion (peeled, chopped)
- 3 garlic cloves (peeled, minced)
- 2 tablespoons tomato paste
- ⅓ cup all-purpose flour
- 4 cups chicken broth (divided)
- 2 bay leaves
- 1 teaspoon dried thyme

Dumplings:

- 2 cups all-purpose flour
- 3 teaspoons baking powder
- 1 teaspoon salt
- ¼ teaspoons pepper
- 1 cup whole milk
- 4 tablespoons butter (melted)

Instructions:

1. Season the chicken with a ¼ teaspoon each of salt and pepper.

2. In the meantime, in a large frying pan or skillet, over moderate to high heat, heat the oil.

3. Add the chicken, and cook while stirring until the chicken is no longer pink, for between 6-8 minutes. Transfer to a slow cooker of 6-quart capacity.

4. Using the same skillet, cook the celery along with the carrots and onions until fork tender, 6-8 minutes.

5. Add the garlic followed by the tomato paste and remaining salt and pepper, cook for 60 seconds.

6. Stir in the flour, cook for an additional 60 seconds.

7. Whisk in 2 cups of broth, cooking and stirring until thickened.

8. Transfer the mixture to the slow cooker and stir in the bay leaves along with the thyme and remaining 2 cups of broth.

9. To prepare the dumplings. In a bowl, whisk the flour with the baking powder, salt, and pepper.

10. Pour in the milk and stir. Add the butter, stirring to make a thick batter.

11. Drop the batter in ¼ cupfuls over the chicken mixture and cook, while covered on low until the mixture is beginning to bubble and the dumplings are set, for 6-8 hours.

12. Remove and discard the bay leaves.

13. Remove the insert and allow to stand for 15 minutes.

Recipe 15: Very Berry Kobbler

Khloe's berry cobbler is a welcome addition to any family meal.

Yield: 6

Preparation Time: 1hour 40mins

Ingredient List:

Fillings:

- 3 (6 ounce) containers fresh blackberries
- 3 (6 ounce) containers fresh blueberries
- 3 (6 ounce) containers fresh raspberries
- ½ cup granulated sugar
- ½ cup packed light brown sugar
- 2 tablespoons cornstarch
- 1 teaspoon ground cinnamon
- Softened butter (to grease)

Topping:

- 2 cups unbleached all-purpose flour
- ⅓ cup + 1 tablespoon granulated sugar
- 1 tablespoon baking powder
- ½ teaspoons salt
- ½ cup cold unsalted butter (cut into small cubes)
- 1 cup heavy cream
- 1 large egg (beaten)
- 2 tablespoons Demerara sugar

HHHHHHHHHHHHHHHHHHHHHHHHHHHHHHHHHHHHHHHHH

Instructions:

1. First, prepare the filling. In a bowl, combine the blackberries with the blueberries, raspberries, granulated sugar, brown sugar, cornstarch, and cinnamon. Take care not to bruise any of the berries. Set aside for half an hour.

2. Preheat the main oven to 350 degrees F. Lightly butter a 9x13" baking dish.

3. To make the topping. In a bowl, whisk the flour with the granulated sugar, baking powder, and salt.

4. Add the butter, tossing to coat with the flour mixture.

5. Using a pastry blender, cut in the butter until a pea-sized, coarse crumbs consistency forms.

6. In a measuring cup, combine the cream with the egg.

7. Stir into the flour mixture until just incorporated.

8. Transfer the filling into the prepared dish.

9. Spoon six, evenly spaced, generous dollops of the topping over the filling.

10. Garnish with coarse sugar.

11. Place the baking dish on a baking sheet and bake in the oven for 40 minutes, until the topping is golden and the filling bubbles. If the topping browns too quickly, using aluminum foil, loosely cover the topping.

12. Serve at room temperature.

Recipe 16: Chicken Quesadillas

Sources reveal that when Robert and Kourtney Kardashian were growing up, they liked nothing more than rice pilaf, lamb chops, and quesadillas. In fact, rumor has it Robert hates anything green!

Yield: 4

Preparation Time: 25mins

Ingredient List:

- 6 ounces refrigerated chicken breast strips (cut into bite size pieces)
- ½ cup store-bought thick and chunky salsa
- 8 (8") flour tortillas for burritos
- Nonstick cooking spray
- 2 cups Colby-Monterey Jack cheese blend
- ¼ cup sour cream

HHHHHHHHHHHHHHHHHHHHHHHHHHHHHHHHHHHHHHHH

Instructions:

1. In a bowl, combine the chicken pieces with the chunky salsa.

2. Spritz one side of each tortilla with nonstick cooking spray.

3. Arrange the sprayed side of each tortilla facing downwards on a 10" non-stick frying pan or skillet.

4. Add ¼ of the chicken-salsa mixture along with ½ cup of the cheese on top of the tortilla. Top with another tortilla. Spritz the top of the tortilla with nonstick spray.

5. Cook over moderate heat, uncovered for 4-6 minutes, flipping over after 2 minutes, until golden.

6. Repeat the process with the remaining tortillas, chicken mixture, and cheese.

7. Cut the quesadillas into wedges and serve with a dollop of sour cream and an extra serving of chunky salsa.

Recipe 17: Turkey Chilli

Enjoy Kourtney's turkey chili with a side order of Kim's cornbread (see recipe on next pages)

Yield: 6

Preparation Time: 1hour

Ingredient List:

- 2 teaspoons olive oil
- 1 yellow onion (peeled, chopped)
- 3 cloves garlic (peeled, minced)
- 1 pound lean ground turkey
- 3 tablespoons chilli powder
- 1 teaspoon dried oregano
- 2 teaspoons ground cumin
- ½ teaspoons salt
- 28 ounces canned diced tomatoes
- 2 (15 ounce) cans kidney beans (drained)
- Avocado, cilantro, and diced onion (to top)

HHHHHHHHHHHHHHHHHHHHHHHHHHHHHHHHHHHHHHHH

Instructions:

1. Over moderate to high heat, add the oil to a large pan.

2. Add the onion along with the garlic and sauté, while frequently stirring for between 5-7 minutes.

3. Next, add the ground turkey. Cook until no longer pink, for approximately 5 minutes.

4. Stir in the chilli powder along with the oregano, cumin, and salt.

5. Finally add the tomatoes together with the kidney beans.

6. Bring to boil, before reducing the heat. Simmer for between 30-45 minutes, until the chili thickens and the flavors meld.

7. Taste the chili and adjust the seasonings.

8. Top with cilantro, avocado, and onion, serve.

Recipe 18: Chocolate Karma Kardashian Cookies

These chocolate cookies are Kourtney's favorite. They are gluten-free, dairy-free and vegan.

Yield: 16

Preparation Time: 1hour 40mins

Ingredient List:

Cookie Dough:

- 3 cups gluten-free flour
- 1¼ cups cocoa powder
- ½ cups tapioca starch
- 2 teaspoons baking soda
- ½ teaspoons salt
- 2 cups organic evaporated cane juice
- 1¼ cups virgin coconut oil (melted before measuring)
- ⅔ cups organic applesauce (warmed)
- 2 teaspoons vanilla essence

Filling:

- ½ cup organic palm shortening
- 2 cups organic powdered sugar (sifted)
- 1 tablespoon almond milk
- ½ teaspoons vanilla essence

HHHHHHHHHHHHHHHHHHHHHHHHHHHHHHHHHHHHHHHH

Instructions:

1. In a bowl, combine the flour with the cocoa powder, starch, baking soda, and salt. Set to one side.

2. In the bowl of a stand food mixer, combine the cane juice with the warmed coconut oil, warm applesauce, and vanilla essence. On a low setting, mix until the sugar is entirely dissolved; this will take between 2-3 minutes.

3. Gradually add in the dry ingredients and on low, mix until the ingredients are incorporated, and the dough comes together.

4. In kitchen wrap, wrap the dough and place in the fridge for 20-30 minutes.

5. Preheat the main oven to 350 degrees F.

6. On a clean work surface, roll the dough out to a ¼" thickness. Cut into 2" circles.

7. Arrange the circles on parchment paper-lined cookie sheets. The circles need to be no more than 1" apart.

8. Bake in the preheated oven for between 7-9 minutes.

9. Remove from the oven and allow to completely cool on a wire baking rack.

10. Next prepare the filling.

11. Attach a whip attachment to your stand mixer, and beat the palm shortening at high speed, for between 3-5 minutes, or until fluffy, light and doubled in size.

12. Gradually add the powdered sugar and milk, mixing until combined. Add the vanilla essence.

13. Once cooled, spoon 1 tablespoon of the cream filling onto half of the cookie sides and cover with the opposing cookie.

14. Transfer to the fridge to set.

Recipe 19: Strawberry, Chocolate and Hazelnut Pizza

Kourtney has a sweet tooth. Although she eats healthily the majority of the time, she also feels it's important to indulge once in a while. This strawberry and chocolate hazelnut pizza is sure to satisfy those sugar cravings.

Yield: 8

Preparation Time: 45mins

Ingredient List:

- Dough:
- 1 teaspoon instant yeast
- ¼ teaspoons sugar
- ¾ cup warm water
- ½ teaspoons salt
- 1 tablespoon olive oil
- 1½-2 cups flour

Topping:

- 1 small banana (peeled, sliced)
- 1 pint strawberries (hulled, sliced)
- 2 tablespoons sliced almonds
- ½ cup chocolate hazelnut spread
- Confectioner's sugar

HHHHHHHHHHHHHHHHHHHHHHHHHHHHHHHHHHHHHHH

Instructions:

1. In a bowl, combine the yeast with the sugar and warm water and allow to sit for 10 minutes.

2. Add the salt and oil with sufficient flour to form a soft dough and allow to rest for 5 minutes. Evenly divide the dough into 2 portions. Roll each portion into a 12" circle.

3. Place on a pizza stone and bake at 500 degrees F for approximately 8-10 minutes, until gently browned.

4. Top each pizza with half of the banana slices, half of the strawberry slices and half of the sliced almonds.

5. In a glass bowl, in the microwave, warm the chocolate hazelnut spread, and then drizzle it over both pizzas.

6. Garnish with confectioner's sugar and serve.

Recipe 20: Homemade Ramen

Khloe enjoys making and eating fresh ramen. It's a comforting dish loaded with veggies, protein-rich chicken, and a softly boiled egg in a salty broth.

Yield: 6

Preparation Time: 45mins

Ingredient List:

- 3 tablespoons canola oil
- 1 medium yellow onion (peeled, coarsely chopped)
- Pinch of salt
- 4 cloves garlic (peeled, finely chopped)
- 1 medium piece of fresh ginger (peeled, chopped)
- 8 cups low-sodium chicken broth
- 4 ounces button mushrooms (cleaned, sliced)
- 3 cups boneless, cooked chicken (shredded)
- Sesame oil
- Low-sodium soy sauce
- 1½ pounds fresh, unseasoned ramen noodles
- 6 soft-boiled eggs (halved)
- 4 green onions, white and light green parts (finely chopped)

HHHHHHHHHHHHHHHHHHHHHHHHHHHHHHHHHHHHHHHH

Instructions:

1. Over moderate to high heat, in a pan, warm 2 tablespoons of oil.

2. Add the onion and lightly season with salt, cooking for 5 minutes, until browned.

3. Stir in the garlic followed by the ginger and broth. Deglaze by scraping any browned bits from the bottom of the pan.

4. Turn the heat down to moderate-low, partially cover the pan and simmer for half an hour.

5. Using a fine mesh sieve, strain the broth, into a mixing bowl.

6. Bring the pan to moderate heat add the remaining oil followed by the mushrooms, continually stirring until fork tender.

7. Add the chicken, stirring to incorporate.

8. Pour in the broth and season with sesame oil.

9. Bring to simmer before reducing the heat to low. Partially cover and simmer for a few minutes.

10. Cook the noodles according to packet instructions.

11. Divide the cooked noodles between 6 bowls, Top each with an equal amount of meat and pour over the broth.

12. Top each with 2 halves of boiled egg, garnish with green onions and serve.

Recipe 21: Kourtney Kardashian's Mac and Cheese with Turkey Bacon

Although Kim holds the Kardashian family crown for her Mac 'n Cheese, Kourtney adds pizzazz to this comforting dish by adding turkey bacon. What's more, her recipe is organic and diet-friendly.

Yield: 8

Preparation Time: 1hour 20mins

Ingredient List:

- 1 (24 ounce) package of gluten-free macaroni noodles
- 6 tablespoons salted butter
- ½ cup organic flour
- 1 teaspoon mustard powder
- 1 teaspoon salt
- 1 teaspoon black pepper
- 5 cups unsweetened almond milk
- 3 cups Pepper Jack cheese (shredded)
- 3 cups cheddar cheese (shredded)
- 8 slices pre-cooked crispy organic turkey bacon (chopped)

HHHHHHHHHHHHHHHHHHHHHHHHHHHHHHHHHHHHHH

Instructions:

1. Pre-heat the main oven to 350 degrees F.

2. Prepare the noodles to al dente. Drain.

3. In a pan melt butter, and add the flour followed by the mustard, salt, pepper, and milk.

4. Stir for 10 minutes until thickened, over moderate heat.

5. Add the cheeses and crispy bacon, stirring to melt entirely.

6. Pour cheese over the drained macaroni, mixing to combine.

7. Transfer to an oven-safe casserole pan and bake until crisp, approximately 45 minutes.

Recipe 22: Khloe's Mash-Up

Next time you crave mashed potatoes, instead go for Khloe's carb-free version, using cauliflower florets.

Yield: 3-4

Preparation Time: 22mins

Ingredient List:

- 1 cup water
- 1 large head cauliflower (broken into florets)
- 1 tablespoon olive oil
- Sea salt
- Freshly ground black pepper
- 1 clove garlic (peeled, chopped)
- Chives (chopped)

HHHHHHHHHHHHHHHHHHHHHHHHHHHHHHHHHHHHHHHHH

Instructions:

1. In a pot, bring 1 cup of water to a simmer. Add the cauliflower florets.

2. Cover the pot with a lid and increase the heat to moderate. Cook until fork-tender, 12-15 minutes. Drain and set aside ¼ cup of the cauliflower cooking water.

3. Add the oil followed by a pinch of salt, a dash of pepper, the garlic, and the chives.

4. Using a potato masher, mash the cauliflower, until it resembles mashed potatoes. You can add the cauliflower cooking water, 1 tablespoon at a time if needed.

Chapter III – Kim

HHHHHHHHHHHHHHHHHHHHHHHHHHHHHHHHHHHHHHHHH

Recipe 23: Fried Dough

Kim Kardashian is a huge fan of fried dough. In fact, while she was pregnant with her son Saint, she made a special trip to Café du Monde in the Crescent City of New Orleans to buy their world famous beignets.

Yield: 18-20

Preparation Time: 40mins

Ingredient List:

- 1 cup all-purpose flour
- 1 teaspoon baking powder
- ⅛ teaspoons kosher salt
- 2 large eggs (separated)
- ¾ cup granulated sugar
- ¼ cup water
- 1 tablespoon butter (melted)
- 1 teaspoon vanilla essence
- Vegetable oil (to fry)
- Confectioner's sugar (to dust)

HHHHHHHHHHHHHHHHHHHHHHHHHHHHHHHHHHHHH

Instructions:

1. In a mixing bowl, whisk the flour with the baking powder and salt.

2. In a second bowl, combine the egg yolks with the sugar, ¼ cup of water, melted butter and vanilla essence to incorporate.

3. Fold the mixture into the dry ingredients until just incorporated.

4. Using a hand mixer, in a bowl, on moderate speed, beat the egg whites until soft peaks begin to form. Fold the mixture into the batter.

5. In a large, deep-sided pot, heat the oil to 375 degrees F.

6. Drop small spoonfuls of the batter into the hot oil and fry for 5 minutes, until golden. The oil needs to be kept at 375 degrees F.

7. Transfer the dough to a plate lined with kitchen paper towel.

8. Dust the fried dough with confectioner's sugar and serve.

Recipe 24: Pine Nut and Rosemary Crusted Lamb

Hollywood gossip columns reveal that when Kim visits her favorite Los Angeles restaurant, she orders rosemary crusted lamb. Now you too can dine like a Kardashian.

Yield: 4

Preparation Time: 40mins

Ingredient List:

- 2 tablespoons fresh rosemary (coarsely chopped)
- ⅓ cup pine nuts (coarsely chopped)
- 1 clove garlic (peeled, crushed)
- 1 cup butter (melted)
- 4 (2-3) riblet racks of lamb (French trimmed)
- Sea salt
- Black pepper

HHHHHHHHHHHHHHHHHHHHHHHHHHHHHHHHHHHHHHH

1. Preheat the main oven to 350 degrees F.

2. Add the fresh rosemary, pine nuts, and garlic to a bowl. Stir in the melted butter and set to one side.

3. Heat a frying pan or skillet, add the racks of lamb and sear on all sides.

4. Transfer the seared lamb to an oven-safe dish.

5. Evenly scatter the pine nut-garlic mixture over the racks of lamb.

6. Roast the lamb in the preheated oven for between 10-15 minutes (medium) or 15-20 minutes for well done.

7. When cooked, remove the lamb from the oven, cover loosely with aluminum foil and set aside to rest for several minutes before serving.

Recipe 25: Chicken Cacciatore

Kim favors a carb-free eating program, and this is one of her favourite recipes.

Yield: 4-6

Preparation Time: 1hour 5mins

Ingredient List:

- 1¼ pounds chicken breast fillets, skin on
- Salt and pepper (to season)
- 3 tablespoons extra virgin olive oil
- ½ cup onions (peeled, chopped)
- 1½ teaspoons garlic (peeled, minced)
- 2 teaspoons rosemary
- 2 ounces Sauvignon Blanc
- ½ teaspoons salt
- ¼ teaspoons crushed red pepper flakes
- 1½ cups whole peeled plum tomatoes

HHHHHHHHHHHHHHHHHHHHHHHHHHHHHHHHHHHHHHH

Instructions:

1. Season the chicken with salt and pepper.

2. In a large frying pan, over moderate to high heat, heat the oil.

3. Add half of the chicken, skin side facing down to the pan and brown for 4 minutes. Flip the chicken over and brown for an additional 4 minutes. Repeat the process with the remaining chicken. Transfer to a plate.

4. Add the onion to the pan along with the minced garlic and rosemary, and cook until the onion softens, 4 minutes.

5. Add the wine to the skillet and bring to boil, continually stirring to help loosen any browned bits from the pan. Sprinkle in the salt and red pepper flakes.

6. Return the chicken to the skillet, skin side facing upwards, along with any of its juices. Cook until the white wine has entirely evaporated, approximately 2 minutes.

7. Next, add the tomatoes. Cover with a lid and turn the heat down to low and simmer for half an hour until the chicken is sufficiently cooked through.

8. Remove the chicken from the pan and place on a platter. Continue to boil the sauce for a couple of minutes, until it begins to thicken.

9. To sever, spoon the sauce over the cooked chicken and serve.

Recipe 26: Mac 'n Cheese, Kim K-Style

According to mum, Kris, Kim's Mac and Cheese is simply the best. One thing is for sure though, she certainly doesn't skimp on the cheese.

Yield: 6

Preparation Time: 50mins

Ingredient List:

- 6 tablespoons butter, plus more for greasing
- 1 pound elbow macaroni
- 3 tablespoons all-purpose flour
- 1 tablespoon dry mustard powder
- 3 cups whole milk (heated)
- ½ yellow onion (peeled, shredded)
- ½ teaspoons sweet paprika
- 1 bay leaf
- 8 ounces processed cheese
- ¼ cup goat cheese (crumbled)
- 1 cup sharp Cheddar cheese (grated)
- ¼ cup mozzarella (grated)
- ¼ cup Gruyere (grated)
- ¼ cup Parmesan (freshly grated)
- Kosher salt
- Freshly ground black pepper
- 3 large eggs (lightly beaten)
- 1 cup panko breadcrumbs

HHHHHHHHHHHHHHHHHHHHHHHHHHHHHHHHHHHHHHHH

Instructions:

1. Preheat the main oven to 350 degrees F.

2. Lightly butter a 9"x13" casserole dish.

3. Cook the macaroni until al dente. Drain well.

4. Over moderate heat, in a large pan, melt 3 tablespoons of butter.

5. Whisk in the flour followed by the mustard.

6. Turn the heat down to low and cook while frequently whisking for a couple of minutes.

7. Whisk in the warmed milk, combining until silky smooth.

8. Whisk in the onion followed by the paprika, and bay leaf.

9. Over moderate heat, bring to simmer while frequently whisking.

10. Increase the heat to moderate and simmer, frequently whisking until the sauce slightly reduces, and has a heavy cream like consistency, approximately 8-10 minutes. Remove from the heat.

11. In a bowl combine the processed cheese, goat cheese, Cheddar, mozzarella, Gruyere, and Parmesan.

12. Add approximately ¾ of the cheese mixture to the sauce and allow to stand for 60 seconds, before stirring to entirely melt the cheese and season.

13. Add the beaten eggs and stir to combine.

14. Next, add the drained macaroni and stir until incorporated.

15. Transfer to the prepared casserole dish and top with the remaining cheese.

16. Over moderate heat, melt the remaining 3 tablespoons of butter. Add the breadcrumbs, stirring well to combine. Sprinkle over the macaroni.

17. Bake the macaroni for half an hour, until the sauce bubbles and the top is golden.

18. Allow to slightly cool for 5 minutes and serve.

Recipe 27: Copycat Take-Out French Fries

Kim's guilty pleasure is a small portion of French fries from a well-known fast food chain. Now you can recreate these golden fries at home.

Yield: 6

Preparation Time: 12hours 45mins

Ingredient List:

- Cold water
- 6 tablespoons white distilled vinegar (divided)
- 2 pounds Idaho potatoes (peeled)
- ½ cup sugar
- Freshly squeezed juice from 1 lemon
- Peanut oil (to fry)
- 1 tablespoon + fine sea salt

HHHHHHHHHHHHHHHHHHHHHHHHHHHHHHHHHHHHHHHH

Instructions:

1. Prepare a cold water bath by combining the 8 cups of water with 2 tablespoons of vinegar.

2. Cut the peeled potatoes into ¼" diameter matchsticks. Add the fries to the vinegar water bath as you work.

3. Take the fries out of the bath and rinse under cold running water.

4. Prepare a second vinegar water bath by combing 8 cups of water with another 2 tablespoons of vinegar. Cover and transfer to the fridge, overnight.

5. The following day, add 4 cups of water along with the sugar in a pan and bring to boil.

[92]

6. Cook until all of the sugar is entirely dissolved, for 60 seconds.

7. Remove the pan from the heat and allow to cool.

8. In a mixing bowl, combine 4 cups of water with the remaining vinegar. Add the lemon juice and mix thoroughly.

9. As soon as the simple syrup is cooled, drain and rinse the potatoes with cold water.

10. Transfer them to a bowl and add the syrup, tossing to combine.

11. Drain the fries from the syrup and then return them to the bowl.

12. Finally toss the fries in the vinegar, water, and lemon juice liquid.

13. Once again, drain the fries and return them to the bowl.

14. In the meantime, in a large frying pan or skillet, heat 4 cups of peanut oil and blanch the fries for between 45-60 seconds.

15. Remove the fries from the peanut oil and arrange on wire cooling rack, shaking vigorously to remove any excess oil.

16. As soon as the fries are sufficiently cool, arrange them in a single layer onto 2 baking sheets, placing them in the freezer for a minimum of 4 hours.

17. Remove the fries from the freezer.

18. In a skillet, heat 4 cups of peanut oil to 275 degrees F.

19. Cook the fries for 5 minutes before removing from the oil. You can work in batches, if necessary.

20. Remove the fries from the oil and turn the heat up to 375 degrees F.

21. Return the fries to the oil and cook for 5 minutes, until crisp and golden.

22. Remove the fries from the oil and arrange on a wire cooling rack, shaking to remove any excess oil.

23. Transfer to a bowl and season with salt, tossing to combine.

24. Enjoy.

Recipe 28: Herbed Hummus

Queen of the Kardashian's Kim enjoys this healthy snack with raw carrot sticks rather than pita bread.

Yield: 6

Preparation Time: 10mins

Ingredient List:

- 4 cups garbanzo beans (drained, rinsed)
- 1 tablespoon agave nectar
- ¼ cup freshly squeezed lemon juice
- 1 teaspoon garlic (peeled, chopped)
- 1 teaspoon cumin
- ⅓ cup extra-virgin olive oil
- ½ bunch cilantro (stemmed)
- 1 tablespoon sea salt
- 1 teaspoon jalapeño (chopped)
- ¼ cup tahini paste
- Carrot sticks (to serve, optional)

HHHHHHHHHHHHHHHHHHHHHHHHHHHHHHHHHHHHHH

Instructions:

1. In a food blender, combine the garbanzo beans with the agave nectar, lemon juice, garlic, cumin, olive oil, cilantro, sea salt, jalapeno and tahini paste, processing until silky smooth.

2. Season to taste and serve with raw carrot sticks.

Recipe 29: Cornbread Muffins

Kim enjoys nothing more than a cornbread muffin. Here, she reveals the secret to achieving a crisp edge on each piece of cornbread. All you have to do is bake them in muffin cups.

Yield: 12

Preparation Time: 30mins

Ingredient List:

- Nonstick cooking spray
- 2 large eggs
- 2 tablespoons pure honey
- ¾ cup whole milk
- 1¼ cups all-purpose flour
- ¾ cup yellow cornmeal
- ¼ cup + 2 tablespoons granulated sugar
- 1 tablespoon baking powder
- 1 teaspoon salt
- ½ cup unsalted melted butter (cooled)

HHHHHHHHHHHHHHHHHHHHHHHHHHHHHHHHHHHHHHH

Instructions:

1. Preheat the main oven to 350 degrees F. Using non-stick cooking spray, spritz a 12-cup muffin pan.

2. Break the eggs, with a whisk, into a bowl.

3. Add the honey, whisking to combine, followed by the milk. Set to one side.

4. In a larger bowl, whisk the flour with the cornmeal, sugar, baking powder and salt.

5. Add the milk mixture together with the melted butter to the dry ingredients, whisking until just blended. Take care not to overmix, even if a few lumps remain.

6. Transfer the mixture into the muffin cups, filling each one to approximately ¾ full.

7. Bake in the preheated oven for between 15-20 minutes, until the tops are set and golden, but not domed.

8. Allow to cool in the muffin cups for 4-6 minutes, before serving.

Recipe 30: Halibut with Asparagus, Spring Onion, and Lemon Thyme

Kim's food diary reveals that she often enjoys this healthy white fish for dinner.

Yield: 4

Preparation Time: 55mins

Ingredient List:

Spring Onions and Asparagus:

- 4 spring onions
- 1 bunch green asparagus
- 1 tablespoon olive oil
- 1 tablespoon shallots (minced)
- 1 teaspoon garlic (peeled, minced)
- 1 tablespoon parsley (minced)
- 2 tablespoons fresh thyme
- Sea salt and freshly ground pepper

Halibut:

- 2 -3 tablespoons extra-virgin olive oil
- 4(6 ounce) halibut fillets
- Sea salt
- 1 tablespoon cold unsalted butter (cold)
- Freshly squeezed juice of 1 lemon (to serve)

HHHHHHHHHHHHHHHHHHHHHHHHHHHHHHHHHHHHH

Instructions:

1. First, prepare the spring onions and asparagus. Hold the asparagus in two hands. One hand just below their tip and the other holding the base, and gently bend until the asparagus snaps.

2. Peel the outside off the asparagus while leaving the tip intact. Securely tie the asparagus, using kitchen twine, together in one bunch.

3. Over high heat, bring a large pan of water to boil. With 1 quart of cold water and 3 cups of ice prepare an ice bath.

4. Add the asparagus to the boiling water, removing when fork tender.

5. Immediately plunge the asparagus into the ice bath and leave in the water for 5 minutes, until cooled.

6. Over moderate-high heat, in a frying pan, heat the oil.

7. Add the spring onions to the pan and cook until golden.

8. Add the blanched asparagus, along with the shallots, garlic, parsley, and thyme. Season to taste.

9. Next, prepare the fish. Preheat the main oven to 350 degrees F.

10. Over high heat, add the olive oil to evenly coat the base of a large frying pan and heat.

11. Season the fish with salt, all over and carefully place in the hot pan.

12. Turn the heat down to moderate and cook on one side until golden. Flip the fish over and add the butter.

13. Add the fish to the oven and cook for a few minutes, until it slightly firms on its sides.

14. When you are ready to serve, spoon the onion and asparagus mixture onto a serving platter. Place the fish on top of the mixture and top with a squeeze of fresh lemon, a drizzle of oil and pinch of sea salt.

15. Enjoy.

Recipe 31: Country Style Pork Ribs

During an interview with BBC Radio 1, Kim admitted she was obsessed with ribs.

Yield: 4

Preparation Time: 2hours

Ingredient List:

- 2½ pounds country-style pork ribs
- Water
- 1 tablespoon garlic powder
- 1 teaspoon ground black pepper
- 2 tablespoons salt
- 1 cup store-bought BBQ sauce

HHHHHHHHHHHHHHHHHHHHHHHHHHHHHHHHHHHHHH

Instructions:

1. Add the ribs to a pot with sufficient water to cover the ribs.

2. Season the ribs with garlic powder, ground black pepper, and salt and bring water to boil, cooking the ribs until tender.

3. Preheat the main oven to 325 degrees F.

4. Take the ribs out of the pot and place them in a 9x13" casserole dish.

5. Pour the BBQ sauce over the ribs.

6. Cover the casserole dish with foil and bake in the oven for between 60-90 minutes, until a meat thermometer registers 160 degrees F.

7. Serve and enjoy.

Chapter IV – Kris

HHHHHHHHHHHHHHHHHHHHHHHHHHHHHHHHHHHHHHHHH

Recipe 32: Wedding Rice Pilaf

This kid-friendly recipe is a firm favorite amongst the grandkids. Its perfect served alongside grilled chicken or lamb chops. In fact, the recipe was passed down from Helen Kardashian, Kris's late ex-husband, Robert.

Yield: 8-10

Preparation Time: 40mins

Ingredient List:

- ½ cup blanched slivered almonds
- 3 tablespoons unsalted butter
- 1½ cups vermicelli (broken into 1½-2" pieces)
- 2 cups long-grain rice
- 3½ cups reduced-sodium chicken broth, heated to steaming
- 1½ teaspoons kosher salt
- ¼ teaspoons freshly ground black pepper
- ½ cup seedless raisins

HHHHHHHHHHHHHHHHHHHHHHHHHHHHHHHHHHHHHH

Instructions:

1. Over moderate heat, heat a skillet.

2. Add the slivered almonds and cook, while occasionally stirring until toasted, this will take a few minutes. Transfer the toasted almonds to a plate and set to one side.

3. Over moderate heat, in a pan, heat the butter.

4. Add the vermicelli and continually stir for 60 seconds, or until lightly toasted.

5. Add the rice, while constantly stirring until the majority of the rice becomes a chalky white, for approximately 60 seconds.

6. Pour in the chicken broth and add the salt and black pepper and over high heat, bring to boil.

7. Turn the heat to moderately low and cover with a tight-fitting lid.

8. Simmer until the rice is tender, and has absorbed the liquid, 16-18 minutes.

9. Remove the rice from the heat and add the toasted almonds and raisins, do not stir to combine. Cover the pan and allow to stand for 5 minutes.

10. With a fork, fluff the pilaf and transfer to a bowl.

11. Serve the pilaf, hot.

Recipe 33: Maple Syrup French Toast

Despite the fact that Kris is a very dedicated dieter, she does admit to yearning after French toast.

Yield: 4

Preparation Time: 10mins

Ingredient List:

- ¾ cup whole milk
- 2 large eggs
- 3 tablespoons pure 100% maple syrup (divided)
- Pinch cinnamon
- Pinch salt
- 2 tablespoons butter
- 4 thick slices Challah bread

HHHHHHHHHHHHHHHHHHHHHHHHHHHHHHHHHHHHHHHH

Instructions:

1. In a bowl, whisk the milk with the eggs, 2 tablespoons maple syrup, cinnamon, and salt.

2. Over moderate heat, melt the butter in a large frying pan or skillet.

3. Soak the Challah bread in the egg batter, making sure that each side is entirely coated.

4. Cook the bread until golden brown, flip over and brown the other side.

5. Repeat this process until all 4 slices are golden brown on both sides.

6. Serve with the remaining maple syrup and enjoy.

Recipe 34: Brownies

Having raised six children, it's no wonder that Kris is a brownie master!

Yield: 20

Preparation Time: 1hour 30mins

Ingredient List:

- All-vegetable shortening (to grease)
- 1 cup unsalted butter (cut into cubes)
- 4 ounces unsweetened baking chocolate (coarsely chopped)
- 1 cup all-purpose flour
- ½ teaspoons baking powder
- ½ teaspoons salt
- 2 cups sugar
- 4 large eggs (room temperature)
- 2 teaspoons vanilla essence
- 2 cups mini semisweet chocolate chips
- 1 cup walnuts (coarsely chopped)

HHHHHHHHHHHHHHHHHHHHHHHHHHHHHHHHHHHHHH

Instructions:

1. Place a rack in the middle of the oven and preheat the main oven to 325 degrees F. Using all-vegetable shortening, grease a 9x13" baking pan.

2. In a large pan over moderate heat, melt the butter. When melted, remove the pan from the heat and add the unsweetened baking chocolate. Allow to stand while the chocolate softens; this will take a few minutes. Stir thoroughly until the chocolate is entirely melted and allow to cool for 5 minutes.

3. In a mixing bowl, combine the flour with the baking powder and salt. Put to one side.

4. In a second bowl, whisk the sugar into the chocolate mixture and one at a time, whisk in the eggs followed by the vanilla essence.

5. Fold in the flour mixture, without using a whisk, until incorporated.

6. Stir in the chocolate chips and chopped walnuts.

7. Transfer the batter into the greased pan, smoothing over the surface with a spatula.

8. Bake until springy to the touch, approximately 20-25 minutes.

9. Transfer the pan to a wire baking rack and allow to cool for 10-12 minutes.

10. Carefully run a knife around the pan's edges to release the brownie and set aside to completely cool while still in the pan.

11. Slice the brownie into 20 evenly sized squares. Remove from the pan and enjoy.

12. Store at room temperature for up to 5 days in an airtight container.

Recipe 35: Turkey and Cheese Enchiladas

Kris readily admits that cooking is one of her main passions and she likes nothing more than to cook for her family. This enchilada recipe using leftover turkey is one of her go-to recipes.

Yield: 6

Preparation Time: 1hour 5mins

Ingredient List:

- 2 tablespoons unsalted butter
- 1 medium yellow onion (peeled, chopped)
- 3 cups cooked turkey (shredded, coarsely chopped)
- 1 (19 ounce) can enchilada sauce (divided)
- 1 (4 ounce) cup sharp Cheddar cheese (shredded, divided)
- 1 (4 ounce) cup Jalapeño Jack cheese (shredded, divided)
- 6 (6") flour tortillas
- ¾ cup sour cream (room temperature)
- Fresh cilantro (chopped, to garnish)

HHHHHHHHHHHHHHHHHHHHHHHHHHHHHHHHHHHHHHH

Instructions:

1. Preheat the main oven to 350 degrees F.

2. Over moderate heat, melt the butter in a frying pan or skillet.

3. Add the onion and cook, while occasionally stirring for 5 minutes, or until translucent.

4. Transfer to a mixing bowl and allow to slightly cool.

5. Stir in the turkey along with ¼ of the enchilada sauce and ½ cup of cheddar cheese and ½ cup of Jalapeno Jack cheese.

6. Evenly spread ½ cup of the enchilada sauce in a 9x13" casserole dish.

7. Pour the remaining enchilada sauce onto a pie plate.

8. Place a tortilla in the sauce.

9. Add approximately ½ a cup of the filling to the middle of the tortilla and neatly roll.

10. Put the rolled enchilada with the seam side facing down in the casserole dish.

11. Repeat the process with the remaining tortillas and filling.

12. Pour any remaining enchilada sauce over the enchiladas and garnish with any remaining cheeses.

13. Bake in the oven until sauce bubbles and the cheese entirely melts, this will take around 20 minutes.

14. Set aside to stand for 5 minutes.

15. Serve hot with a generous dollop of sour cream and garnished with cilantro.

Recipe 36: Chicken Vodka Pasta

When matriarch of the famous Kardashian dynasty visits New York she loves visiting her favorite restaurant where she tucks into this vodka-infused pasta dish.

Yield: 4

Preparation Time: 55mins

Ingredient List:

- 4 tablespoons olive oil
- 12 ounces chicken breast (cut into bite-size pieces)
- Salt and black pepper
- 1 small onion (peeled, finely chopped)
- 2 garlic cloves (peeled, minced)
- ½ cup vodka
- 1 (28 ounce) can Italian crushed tomatoes
- 1 teaspoon granulated garlic
- 1 teaspoon granulated onion
- ½ teaspoons dried basil
- 1 teaspoon dried oregano
- Pinch of hot pepper flakes
- ½ cup heavy cream
- 12 ounces penne
- Fresh basil
- ½ cup Parmigiano Reggiano (freshly grated)

HHHHHHHHHHHHHHHHHHHHHHHHHHHHHHHHHHHHHHHH

Instructions:

1. In a high sided skillet, add 2 tablespoons of oil and preheat over moderately high heat.

2. Add the chicken, season and sauté until browned. Set to one side.

3. Over moderate heat and in the same pan, fry the onion in the remaining oil for between 4-5 minutes.

4. Next, add the garlic and fry for 60 seconds.

5. Pour in the vodka and cook until it has reduced by approximately 50 percent.

6. Add the tomatoes along with the granulated garlic and onion followed by the basil, oregano and pepper flakes.

7. Turn the heat down to moderate-low and while partially covered, and frequently stirring, cook for 40 minutes.

8. In the meantime, fill a deep sided pan with water, add a generous pinch of salt and bring to boil.

9. When 40 minutes have elapsed, season the sauce and add the heavy cream along with the browned partially cooked chicken. You can also add any juice that has collected on the plate.

10. Increase the heat to moderate and while uncovered, cook for 6-8 minutes.

11. Add the penne to the boiling water and cook until al dente.

12. Drain the penne and add it to the vodka sauce.

13. Turn off the heat and add the basil leaves together with the grated cheese. Stir to incorporate and serve.

Recipe 37: Sweet Potato Soufflé

A firm Kardashian-Jenner favorite, this sweet potato soufflé is always a part of every family holiday meal.

Yield: 10-12

Preparation Time: 1hour 35mins

Ingredient List:

- 6 sweet potatoes (each potato cut into 4)
- 1 cup butter (melted)
- 1 pound brown sugar
- 2 cups white sugar
- 1 (14 ounce) can sweetened condensed milk
- 1 teaspoon vanilla essence
- 1 teaspoon cinnamon
- 1 teaspoon nutmeg
- 6 medium eggs (finely beaten)

HHHHHHHHHHHHHHHHHHHHHHHHHHHHHHHHHHHHHHH

Instructions:

1. Boil the sweet potatoes for 20 minutes, until fork tender.

2. Peel and mash the potatoes until very fine. Add the butter along with the brown sugar, white sugar, condensed milk, vanilla essence, cinnamon, and nutmeg.

3. Finally, add the beaten eggs and transfer the mixture to a soufflé dish.

4. Bake the soufflé in the main oven at 375 degrees F for 60 minutes.

Recipe 38: Hearty Chicken Soup

In the fall, as the weather gets a little cooler, Kris serves this soup with crunchy French bread.

Yield: 8-10

Preparation Time: 2hours 30mins

Ingredient List:

Stock:

- 2 medium-size rotisserie chickens
- 6 cups water
- 1 medium-size yellow onion (peeled, cut into quarters)
- 1 medium-size carrot (coarsely chopped)
- 1 medium-size celery rib (coarsely chopped)
- Salt and black pepper (to taste)

Soup:

- 2 medium-size celery ribs (cut into ½" dice)
- 2 medium-size carrots (cut into ½" dice)
- 2 cups bite-size broccoli florets
- 3 large scallions, white and green parts (thinly sliced)
- 1 medium-size squash (cut into ½" dice)
- 1 medium-size zucchini (cut into ½" dice)
- 1 teaspoon cumin
- 1 teaspoon chili powder
- 1 teaspoon all-purpose seasoning salt
- ¼ cup pearled barley
- 1 cup pastina pasta
- Crusty French bread (to serve)

Instructions:

1. Remove the meat from the chicken and shred and chop into bite-sized pieces. Cover and transfer to the fridge to add to the soup later.

2. In a large soup pot combine the chicken skin and its carcass along with 6 cups of water, the onion, carrot and celery rib.

3. Over moderate heat, cook for 60 minutes, skimming off any surface foam.

4. Using a colander, strain the stock into a mixing bowl. Remove and discard any solids. Season to taste.

5. To prepare the soup, return the stock to the soup pot.

6. Add the chicken, celery, carrots, broccoli florets, scallions, squash, zucchini, cumin, chili powder, seasoning salt, and pearled barley. Simmer for 60 minutes.

7. Finally, add the pasta and cook for a further 10-12 minutes, adding a drop of water to thin the consistency if required.

8. Serve hot with crusty bread.

Recipe 39: Pasta Primavera

Kris's Pasta Primavera is another family favorite. Packed full with fresh veggies it's super easy to make and very healthy.

Yield: 4-6

Preparation Time: 45mins

Ingredient List:

- 16 ounces bow tie pasta
- ¼ cup extra-virgin olive oil
- 2 large carrots (cut into ½" dice)
- ½ head broccoli (snapped into small florets)
- 1 zucchini (halved lengthwise, cut into ¼" thick half-moons)
- 1 red bell pepper (cored, seeded, cut into ¼" wide strips)
- 1 yellow bell pepper (cored, seeded, cut into ¼" wide strips)
- 1 green bell pepper (cored, seeded, cut into ¼" wide strips)
- 1 garlic clove (peeled, minced)
- Kosher salt and freshly ground black pepper
- ½ cup Parmesan cheese (freshly grated)
- ¼ cup fresh basil (chopped)
- Parmesan cheese (freshly grated, to serve)

HHHHHHHHHHHHHHHHHHHHHHHHHHHHHHHHHHHHHHHH

Instructions:

1. Cook the pasta in a pan of boiling salted water until al dente.

2. In the meantime, over moderate heat, in a large frying pan or skillet, heat the oil.

3. Add the carrots and cover with a lid, and cook while occasionally stirring until the carrot are fork-tender, 5 minutes.

4. Add the broccoli along with the zucchini and cook, while uncovered, occasionally stirring for an additional 3 minutes, until they soften.

5. Add the red, yellow and green peppers and cook while frequently stirring until fork tender, 5 minutes.

6. During the final 2-3 minutes, stir in the garlic and season to taste. Remove the skillet from the heat and partially cover with a lid to ensure the veggies remain warm.

7. When the pasta is al dente, drain and set ½ a cup of the pasta cooking liquid to one side.

8. Return the pasta to its pot and add the veggies along with the cheese and basil, mixing well to combine. Add a sufficient amount of pasta cooking water to melt the cheese and form a light sauce. Season to taste.

9. Serve hot with extra grated Parmesan on the side.

Recipe 40: Lemon Cake

While daughter Khloe loves to cook from scratch, busy entrepreneur mum, Kris, makes her famous lemon cake using an instant pudding mix.

Yield: 12-16

Preparation Time: 1hour 35mins

Ingredient List:

- 1 (serves 4) pack lemon instant pudding mix
- 1 cup cold water
- 4 organic eggs

Glaze:

- 1 cup confectioner's sugar
- 2 tablespoons freshly squeezed lemon juice.

HHHHHHHHHHHHHHHHHHHHHHHHHHHHHHHHHHHHHH

Instructions:

1. Preheat the main oven to 350 degrees F.

2. In a food blender on moderate speed beat the pudding mix with the water and eggs for 2 minutes.

3. Transfer the mixture to a greased and lightly floured 10" fluted pan and bake in the oven for 45-55 minutes, until springy to the touch.

4. Remove from the oven and cool while still in the pan for half an hour, before inverting onto a plate.

5. Poke evenly spaced holes in the cake and drizzle with the glaze.

6. To make the glaze, in a bowl, combine the confectioner's sugar with the fresh lemon juice.

About the Author

Angel Burns learned to cook when she worked in the local seafood restaurant near her home in Hyannis Port in Massachusetts as a teenager. The head chef took Angel under his wing and taught the young woman the tricks of the trade for cooking seafood. The skills she had learned at a young age helped her get accepted into Boston University's Culinary Program where she also minored in business administration.

Summers off from school meant working at the same restaurant but when Angel's mentor and friend retired as head chef, she took over after graduation and created classic and new dishes that delighted the diners. The restaurant flourished under Angel's culinary creativity and one customer developed more than an appreciation for Angel's food. Several months after taking over the position, the young woman met her future husband at work and they have been inseparable ever since. They still live in Hyannis Port with their two children and a cocker spaniel named Buddy.

Angel Burns turned her passion for cooking and her business acumen into a thriving e-book business. She has authored several successful books on cooking different types of dishes using simple ingredients for novices and experienced chefs alike. She is still head chef in Hyannis Port and says she will probably never leave!

Author's Afterthoughts

With so many books out there to choose from, I want to thank you for choosing this one and taking precious time out of your life to buy and read my work. Readers like you are the reason I take such passion in creating these books.

It is with gratitude and humility that I express how honored I am to become a part of your life and I hope that you take the same pleasure in reading this book as I did in writing it.

Can I ask one small favour? I ask that you write an honest and open review on Amazon of what you thought of the book. This will help other readers make an informed choice on whether to buy this book.

My sincerest thanks,

Angel Burns

If you want to be the first to know about news, new books, events and giveaways, subscribe to my newsletter by clicking the link below

https://angel-burns.gr8.com

or Scan QR-code

59712055R00081